Tadpole Books are published by Jump!, 5357 Penn Avenue South, Minneapolis, MN 55419, www.jumplibrary.com

Copyright ©2020 Jump!. International copyright reserved in all countries. No part of this book may be reproduced in any form without written permission from the publisher.

Editor: Jenna Trnka **Designer:** Anna Peterson **Translator:** Annette Granat

Photo Credits: Michiel de Wit/Shutterstock, cover; Tony Campbell/Shutterstock, 1; Jay Ondreicka/Shutterstock, 2tr, 3; Ivan Kuzmin/Alamy, 2br, 4–5; age fotostock/SuperStock, 2tl, 6–7; Clara Bastian/Shutterstock, 2ml, 8–9; PRILL/Shutterstock, 2bl, 10–11; Terry Whittaker Wildlife/Alamy, 2mr, 12–13; Eric Isselee/Shutterstock, 14–15; Ivan Kuzmin/Shutterstock, 16.

Library of Congress Cataloging-in-Publication Data
Names: Nilsen, Genevieve, author.
Title: Las ranas / Genevieve Nilsen.
Other titles: Frogs. Spanish
Description: Tadpole books edition. | Minneapolis, MN: Jump!, Inc., (2020) | Series: Animales en tu jardín | Includes index. | Audience: Ages 3–6
Identifiers: LCCN 2019041578 (print) | LCCN 2019041579 (ebook) | ISBN 9781645272618 (hardcover) | ISBN 9781645272625 (paperback) ISBN 9781645272632 (ebook)
Subjects: LCSH: Frogs—Juvenile literature.
Classification: LCC QL668.E2 N5518 2020 (print) | LCC QL668.E2 (ebook) | DDC 597.8/9—dc23

ANIMALES EN TU JARDÍN
LAS RANAS

por Genevieve Nilsen

TABLA DE CONTENIDO

Palabras a saber..........................2
Las ranas................................3
¡Repasemos!............................16
Índice..................................16

PALABRAS A SABER

comen

croan

huevos

nadan

renacuajos

saltan

LAS RANAS

Las ranas croan.

Las ranas saltan.

Las ranas comen insectos.

Los huevos de las ranas están en el agua.

Los renacuajos nadan.

Ellos crecen.

¡REPASEMOS!

¿Qué está haciendo esta rana?

ÍNDICE

agua 9
comen 7
croan 3
huevos 9, 11

insectos 7
nadan 13
renacuajos 11, 13
saltan 5